Wise Words for Boys -
31 Days of Proverbs

To: Abril & all the young men that follow you in your generations

From Evangelist Delores P. Scott

your beloved Auntie

Wise Words for Boys -
31 Days of Proverbs

Denia Petruzella

WestBow
PRESS
A DIVISION OF THOMAS NELSON

WestBow Press books may be ordered through booksellers or by contacting:

WestBow Press
A Division of Thomas Nelson
1663 Liberty Drive
Bloomington, IN 47403
www.westbowpress.com
1-(866) 928-1240

Because of the dynamic nature of the Internet, any web addresses or links contained in this book may have changed since publication and may no longer be valid. The views expressed in this work are solely those of the author and do not necessarily reflect the views of the publisher, and the publisher hereby disclaims any responsibility for them.

Any people depicted in stock imagery provided by Thinkstock are models, and such images are being used for illustrative purposes only.

Certain stock imagery © Thinkstock.

ISBN: 978-1-4497-3828-0 (sc)
ISBN: 978-1-4497-3827-3 (hc)
ISBN: 978-1-4497-3829-7 (e)

Library of Congress Control Number: 2012901273

Printed in the United States of America

WestBow Press rev. date: 1/31/2012

To my sons, Michael and Anthony,
I love you.

Table of Contents

Preface

When reading the Book of Proverbs in my own personal Bible study, I couldn't help but notice the many references made to "young men." The author of most of Proverbs and one of the wisest men to ever have lived, King Solomon, sought to share his wisdom with his sons and all generations of young men to follow. He wanted them to learn from his education, experience, observations, and, most important, his mistakes. Since I have two young boys of my own, the verses began to take on a very special significance for me. King Solomon's wisdom was given to him as a gift from God. He was not born wise; he asked for it, as is explained further in the introduction. His God-inspired writings have been relevant for hundreds of years, as is every verse in the Bible. I have merely captured some of the most meaningful proverbs for my family and hope that they are helpful to you and your sons as well.

This is a thirty-one-day devotion book. Each day includes the main topical scripture from the Book of Proverbs and a short discussion of the subject that is suitable for boys of all ages. I then include a list of scriptures that could be used in the discussion should you want to delve deeper into study with your child. Next is a prayer to say with your child, and finally, a "Walk the Walk" or "Talk the Talk" segment provides parents with ideas for being the role models we should strive to be for our sons. Proverbs 22:6 says, "Train up a child in the way he should go, Even when he is old he will not depart from it" (New American Standard Bible [NASB]). It is my hope that this book might help in some small way in training our boys to grow into strong, Christian men.

Please read the Introduction to your child so he will understand the story behind the daily proverbs.

Introduction

In Psalm 119:9–10, King David said: "How can a young man keep his way pure? By keeping it according to Your (God's) word" (NASB). As we all know, David was "a man after [God's] own heart." (Acts 13:22 NASB) Of course, he made mistakes, as all humans do, but he truly loved the Lord with all his heart, mind, and soul. In this psalm, David is telling all of us—in particular, young men—that the only way to be successful in life (according to God's standards, not man's) is to know the word of God and keep His commandments. If you succeed in that endeavor, you will remain pure and righteous in God's eyes.

After the glorious reign of King David was over, his young son Solomon was ordained by God to be king over Israel and Judah. God came to Solomon in a dream and told him that he could ask for any one thing and it would be granted to him. Solomon told God that he was young and inexperienced, so he requested that God give him wisdom to rule over the people. God was pleased and so impressed with Solomon that He granted him not only wisdom but also all the things he could have wished for but didn't: riches, glory, victory over enemies, and so on. God told him all these things would be his if he followed God's commandments. Solomon went on to be not only wise but possibly the richest king in all of history. His kingdom experienced peace and prosperity during the entirety of his reign as a result of his God-given wisdom.

Solomon used the teachings of his father David, his life experiences, and the wisdom granted to him by God Himself to write hundreds of proverbs. As all scripture is inspired by God, the proverbs written by Solomon speak to each and every one of us today, being just as applicable to modern life situations as they were three thousand years ago. They are words of wisdom that we would all do well to live by. Many of the proverbs are directed specifically to young men. This book is a compilation of thirty-one proverbs, as well as other scriptures from the Old and New Testaments, designed especially to be shared with your sons.

There is no better introduction to this book than Solomon's own introduction to the Book of Proverbs. Chapter 1:1–4 says, "The Proverbs of Solomon the son of David, king of Israel: to know wisdom and instruction, to discern the sayings of understanding, to receive instruction in wise behavior, righteousness, justice and equity; to give prudence to the naive, to the youth knowledge and discretion." (NASB)

Day 1: Fear God

Proverbs 1:7 (NASB): "The fear of the Lord is the beginning of knowledge; Fools despise wisdom and instruction." Proverbs 9:10–11 (NASB): "The fear of the Lord is the beginning of wisdom, and the knowledge of the Holy One is understanding. For by me your days will be multiplied, and years of life will be added to you."

What does it mean to fear God? Are you supposed to be afraid of Him? Well, yes. He is all-powerful and all-knowing. God holds our eternal fate in His hands. God judges every human being after death and decides who will enter into heaven or be sent to hell at the end of time. But the word *fear* in these verses also means "to respect and honor." God is the creator of the universe: our planet and all plants, animals, and people—including you. God created us and our world for His pleasure. God created you as a special person and for a special purpose—to love and obey Him.

You should also respect and give honor to God because He loves you! In fact, God loves you so much that He sent His only Son, Jesus, to die for you so that you might be saved.

After experiencing fortune and fame, love, marriage (to many women), children, power, and the fulfillment of every desire throughout his lifetime, King Solomon wrote about the meaning of life in his book Ecclesiastes. He concluded his book with one profound, final statement and the most important lesson he learned from all of his life experiences: "Let us hear the conclusion of the whole matter: Fear God, and keep his commandments: for this is the whole duty of man." (Eccl. 12:13 King James Version [KJV]) Solomon tells us that the whole purpose of man is to fear God and keep His commandments. You were created by God to fear, respect, honor, and obey Him. The entire reason that human beings exist on the earth and have since God created it is to fear, honor, worship, and obey God. Your purpose here in this world is to glorify God. Now you know the meaning of life!

1

It is simple. If you want to be smart, the first and most important thing you will learn is to fear and respect God. This is the beginning of true wisdom.

References: Psalm 139:13–16   John 3:16   Ecclesiastes 12:13
              Deuteronomy 13:4

Prayer: Almighty God in heaven, I love you and I fear you. I praise you for creating our beautiful world. Thank you for making me especially for you and for your purpose. Help me to learn of you and your precious Son, Jesus. Let me honor you today in all that I say and do. In Christ's name I pray, amen.

Parents, Talk the Talk: Do you demonstrate respect for God to your son(s) in your everyday speech? Do you use the name of God or Jesus as part of slang, as an expression, when you are angry or telling jokes? The third of the Ten Commandments says, "You shall not take the name of the Lord your God in vain, for the Lord will not leave him unpunished who takes his name in vain" (Exodus 20:7 NASB). We should teach our children that modern-day phrases such as "Oh, my God!" ("OMG" in cyber talk) are taking the name of the Lord in vain and do not show respect.

Day 2: Choose Your Friends Wisely

Proverbs 1:10 and 15 (NASB): "My son, if sinners entice you, do not consent." "My son, do not walk in the way with them. Keep your feet from their path."

Have you ever found yourself being punished because you were with a friend who was doing something wrong and you followed along and joined in? Think about it. If you had been alone or possibly with another friend, would you have done or said the things that got you into trouble? Every young man makes mistakes sometimes, but if you have a friend who *consistently* behaves badly around you, who mistreats or bullies you or others, breaks rules at home or at school, or is disrespectful to his or her parents or teachers, you should seriously reconsider hanging out with that person. This kind of friend will get you into trouble.

The Bible tells us that we should choose friends who have the same beliefs in God and Jesus that we do. The apostle Paul said, "Don't team up with those who are unbelievers. How can goodness be a partner with wickedness? How can light live with darkness?" (2 Cor. 6:14 New Living Translation [NLT]).

Because you live in this world, you will have to interact with non-Christians every day, at school, at extracurricular activities, and in your neighborhood. But, that doesn't mean that you have to be best friends with them. There is a famous saying: "Birds of a feather flock together." This means that people with the same type of personality are naturally attracted to each other. If you are hanging out with mean-spirited kids or troublemakers, what does that say about your walk with Jesus? You can seek out and find good young men to befriend—fellow Christians who will not lead you down the wrong path. When your closest friends are also believers, it is easier for you to resist temptation. You want to hang out with good "birds," not ones who are constantly in trouble and will take you down with them.

References: 2 Corinthians 6:14–15   Romans 12:10   James 4:4

Prayer: God, you are awesome, and I praise you for all the blessings of friendship. Please guide me and help me to choose my companions wisely. Please strengthen me to resist the temptation to associate with people who do not follow you, even though they may be popular. And when I am in the company of nonbelievers, please help me to be a good influence on them. Thank you for giving me the greatest friend of all—Jesus. It is in His name I pray, amen.

Parents, Walk the Walk: Have you made friends with other Christian parents at your church? Does your son see you enjoying the company of fellow Christians? If you have not done so already, make the time and effort to develop friendships with fellow Christians. Stay for fellowship meals or other after-church activities. Allow your son to hang out and go on outings with his Christian peers. Not only is it important for your son to have guy friends in the church, but one day you will want him to have a girlfriend who is a Christian also.

Day 3: Obey the Commandments of God and Jesus

Proverbs 2:1, 5, 6 (NASB): "My son, if you will receive my words and treasure my commandments within you, then you will discern the fear of the Lord and discover the knowledge of God. For the Lord gives wisdom; from His mouth come knowledge and understanding."

Laws, rules, and guidelines are put to use every day, everywhere you go, and in all that you do. Could you imagine going to a school with no rules or playing football, baseball, soccer, or even checkers without any rules? Without laws, guidelines, and rules, our world would be a mess. The same is true with God's rules. Commandments are the rules that God gives us to live by. If there were no commandments to follow, Christians would not know what is right and what is wrong behavior.

A man once asked Jesus what the most important commandment was. Jesus answered, "The most important one is, 'Love the Lord your God with all your heart, and with all your soul, and with all your mind and with all your strength.' The second is this, 'Love your neighbor as yourself.' There is no commandment greater than these" (Matt. 22:37,39 NASB). If every person in the world would follow just these two rules, there would be no war, murder, robbery, slander, lying, cheating, or any other sin.

Jesus also said, "If you love Me, you will keep My commandments" (John 14:15 NASB). Of course we love Jesus. We love Him because He first loved us and He gave Himself as a sacrifice for us. However, we *prove* our love to God and Jesus by keeping their commandments. The apostle John said, "For this is the love of God, that we keep His commandments; and His commandments are not burdensome" (I John 5:3 NASB). When you love God, you *want* to keep His commandments; you *want* to follow His rules for your life.

What are the commandments and rules you should follow, and where do you find them? The Bible is the direct word of God to His children. It is the rule book for your life. First, you must follow the two most important commandments as identified by Jesus above. Then, begin studying His word. The Ten Commandments in the Old Testament, given to Moses for the children of Israel to follow, were also carried over to the New Testament (with the exception of the Sabbath; Christians worship on Sunday), and you should know them as well. In addition to these, there are many other commandments given to Christians in the New Testament, including those concerning the plan of salvation. You should learn and follow them all.

References: Mark 12:28–31   1 John 4:19   John 14:15
        1 John 5:3   Exodus 20: 1–17

Prayer: My holy God, I praise you for loving me, even when I break your rules. Help me to show my love for you by following your commandments. Thank you for sending the Word to us: your Son and the Bible. Help me to seek your will and study my Bible so that I know the things you want me to do. In Jesus' precious name I pray, amen.

Parents, Walk the Walk: Does your son see you reading and studying your Bible every day, every week, ever? If not, get your Bible out and help him with this challenge. Over the next ten days, go over the Ten Commandments (Ex. 20:1–17) with your son and then try to find ten other commandments spoken by either Jesus or one of His disciples in the New Testament. Write them down and post them as a reminder to follow God's rules. Set the example. If he sees you reading the Bible, he will be more likely to do so himself.

Day 4: Trust God

Proverbs 3: 5– 6 (NASB): "Trust in the Lord with all your heart and do not lean on your own understanding. In all your ways acknowledge Him, and He will make your paths straight."

At some point in your life, you will be faced with a serious problem, a terrible disappointment, or a heartbreaking loss. Things may happen to you, your family, or your friends that you do not understand. Someone you love may become ill or die. One of your parents may lose a job or takes a job that requires you to move far away from your family and friends. You or loved ones may suffer because of a fire, tornado, or other disaster. Or you may have a friend who betrays you and breaks your heart. All human beings, young and old, endure troubles, heartaches, and even catastrophes from time to time.

When something awful happens, you may want to ask, "Why? Why did this happen to me (or my friend or my loved one)?" Your parents or your preacher will not always have the answer. But God does. The Bible calls these occurrences "trials" and tells us how to deal with them. God has a plan for your life and everything that happens to you. Romans 8:28 (NLT) says, "And we know that God causes everything to work together for the good of those who love God and are called according to his purpose for them." If you love God and trust Him, then everything that happens—good or bad—will turn out for the best. It may take a while, even years possibly, to see the results, but God knows the purpose of that trial in your life, and He will use it for your good.

God is always there to comfort you. He will never leave you or desert you. God loves you so much, and He wants you to lean on Him whenever you are faced with a trial in life. When you were little and you scraped your knee, do you remember running to your mom or dad and letting them hug you and tell you everything would be all right? Did that make you feel better? Now that you are older, God wants you to run to Him with your troubles. He is your heavenly Father. When you are feeling down, lonely, hurt, or heartbroken, He is there to comfort you and to tell you everything will be all right. If you love God, then you must trust God to work all things together for your good.

References: James 1:2–8   Jeremiah 29:11–13   Psalm 9:9–10
              Romans 8:14,16–17

Prayer: Dear heavenly Father, thank you for loving me and taking care of me. Please help me to come to you when I am sad or hurt or have a problem. Please help me to trust you to make everything (even the bad things) work for good according to your will and plan for my life. I know that I do not have the answers to all of life's problems, but you do. Thank you for letting me be your child. In Jesus Christ's name I pray, amen.

Parents, Talk the Talk: Does your son see or hear you complaining or distressing over trials in your life? Does he see or hear you praying to God for His comfort in your times of need? Set the example when things go wrong; pray first, and then trust God to make all things work together for good.

Day 5: Give Back to God

Proverbs 3:9 (NASB): "Honor the Lord from your wealth and from the first of all your produce."

If someone were to ask you, "Where did you get your home, food, clothing, and other possessions?" you would probably say, "From my parents." That would be true; however, it is God who put you in this amazingly rich and prosperous country and who gave your parents their talents and the opportunity to work and provide for you. Everything we have comes from God and ultimately belongs to God. We are merely using this "stuff" here on earth for a time.

Because God has so richly blessed us in so many ways, He expects us to give back to Him to show our love, gratitude, and thankfulness. Thousands of years ago, when God's people followed the law of Moses, they were required to offer the first and best fruits from their crops and animals as an offering to God. Today, even though New Testament Christians are not required to offer animal or food sacrifices to God, He still expects us to give our best back to Him—our "first-fruits," as they were called in the Old Testament. So, how do we do this?

There are many ways we can honor God by giving back to Him. Every week, an opportunity is given in church services to make a monetary offering to the Lord. God expects you to decide in advance how much you will give. The money you give should come out of your allowance first, not what is left over at the end of the week. There are also homeless shelters, food pantries, foster homes, hospitals, and missionaries who can use donations of your food, clothing, and money. When you give to your church or to help others in need, you are actually giving back to God. Proverbs 19:17 says, "One who is gracious to a poor man lends to the Lord, and He will repay him for his good deed" (NASB).

Another valuable commodity, or "first-fruit," that you have and can give back to the Lord is your time. You should make time every day to pray, study your Bible, and talk about God and Jesus with your family and friends. And remember, when you give back to God, it must be done with a happy heart. Your offering of money, time, or anything else is not pleasing to Him if it is given grudgingly or with a bad attitude. God has given you so much that you should be happy to give your first-fruits of everything to the Lord.

References: 2 Corinthians 9:6–11   Deuteronomy 15:7–11   Acts 20:35

Prayer: My holy Father, the blessings of this life are too numerous to count. Thank you not only for giving me all the things I need—my home, food, and clothing—but for the way you lavish me with so many comforts and material goods. Please, Lord, help me to be a cheerful giver of my money and my time to you. Lord, I give you all the glory and honor for all that I have. Thank you, God, for giving me the greatest blessing of all—your Son. It is in His name that I pray, amen.

Parents, Walk the Walk: Do you set aside a certain amount each week to give to God, or do you wait to see how much is left over after all the bills are paid? Does your son see you giving with a happy heart? If you do not give your child a weekly allowance, consider doing so, if for no other reason than that he can begin giving a portion of his own money to God each week at church.

Day 6: Punishment Equals Love

Proverbs 3:11-12 (NASB): "My son, do not reject the discipline of the Lord or loathe His reproof, for whom the Lord loves He reproves, even as a father corrects the son in whom he delights."

Why do your parents punish you when you break a rule or disobey them? They do it because they love you. Sometimes that doesn't make sense to young people. You might think they are just being mean or that they enjoy hurting you, but that is not true. A parents' job is hard. They are responsible for keeping you safe; providing a home, clothing, and food for you; teaching you the difference between right and wrong; giving you lots of love and affection; and helping you in every way to grow up to be a Christian adult. The Bible tells parents to bring their children up in the discipline and instruction of the Lord, and the Bible tells children that a parent who disciplines them loves them.

God disciplines His children when they do wrong, and God expects parents to discipline their children when they do wrong. God disciplines out of love, and so do your parents. Many of the rules your parents set are made to keep you safe; they don't want you to get hurt. Other rules teach you how to behave with respect for adults, your family, and your peers. Your parents set boundaries, establish rules, and tell you no because they know what is best for you.

Your parents do not enjoy punishing you when you disobey. However, if there were no consequences for bad behavior, then there would be no reason for you to stop doing things that are wrong. The next time your parents punish you, you must respect their authority and remember that they do it out of love and concern for you. They are doing their job as parents. When you are punished, learn the lesson they are trying to teach you and try not to make the same mistake again. If you learn from your mistake, then your punishment has served the purpose that God intended. The more you learn about obeying rules as a child, the fewer mistakes you will make as an adult.

References: Ephesians 6:1–4   Hebrews 12:4–11

Prayer: Dear God, thank you for being my spiritual Father and for giving me loving parents who take care of me, protect me, and discipline me when I do wrong. Please help me to respect my parents and obey them. Thank you for the Bible and all the guidance you give me and my parents from your Word. Please help me to learn from my mistakes and try to do my best to follow the rules my parents have set. In Jesus' holy name I pray, amen.

Parents, Walk the Walk: Are you consistent in the discipline of your children? Do you let them get away with something one day and punish them for that same behavior the next day? Kids need discipline that fits the crime, and it should always be consistent to be effective.

Day 7: Stay Focused

Proverbs 4:25–26 (NASB): "Let your eyes look directly ahead and let your gaze be fixed straight in front of you. Watch the path of your feet and all your ways will be established."

Have you ever participated in a race? If so, your coach probably told you something along the lines of the words found in this proverb: "Look directly ahead and keep your eyes on the finish line." The coach knows that if you are running and you look all around or behind you, you will become distracted and lose speed. But if you stay focused on the finish line in front of you, not looking to the side or behind you, you will get there much faster. God is much wiser than any human coach. He wants you to be focused on Jesus as you go about your daily race so that you can accomplish His will for your life. Of course, you have to prepare for and think about important things like schoolwork, tests, church, sports, and other activities you are involved in. However, you must stay focused on Jesus in order to please God.

How do you juggle the activities of life while still staying focused on Jesus? The apostle Paul compares daily life with running a race. He says that we must run with endurance to reach the prize, which is eternal life with Jesus. One way you can accomplish this is by praying several times a day, not only at mealtime or at bedtime. Each time you are presented with a situation or a question and are unsure about how to respond, or you have an important test to take or activity to participate in, talk to Jesus about it. Ask Him for His answer to the problem or question, His guidance, and His help.

Another great way to stay focused on Jesus is by reading the Bible every day. Jesus gives the answers to so many of life's situations in His teachings and parables. He tells us that the only way to get to heaven someday is by knowing Him and obeying His commandments. The only way to do that is by studying His word.

The apostle Paul also tells us that we should put all our past mistakes behind us. It is hard to live each new day for Jesus when you are worried about something bad from the past. When you ask Jesus for His forgiveness, He gives it—completely. He also wipes it away from all memory, and you should too. Each new day is like participating in a new race. You have the opportunity to run with your eyes fixed straight ahead, staying focused on Jesus, the grand prize!

References: Hebrews 12:1–3   John 14:21   Philippians 3:7–16

Prayer: Dear Lord, I love you for giving me your Son, Jesus, to be my perfect example. Help me to live each day for Him, staying focused on His word and His will for my life. Help me to obey your commandments so that I may reach the final prize—eternal life in heaven. In Jesus' name I pray, amen.

Parents, Walk the Walk: Do you fix your eyes on Jesus every day, or do the worries and responsibilities of life distract you? Let your son see you reading the Bible every day and praying to God for His guidance with daily problems.

Day 8: Be Humble

Proverbs 6:16–19 (NASB): "There are six things which the LORD hates, yes, seven which are an abomination to Him: haughty eyes, a lying tongue, and hands that shed innocent blood, a heart that devises wicked plans, feet that run rapidly to evil, a false witness who utters lies, and one who spreads strife among brothers." Proverbs 21:4 (NLT): "Haughty eyes, a proud heart, and evil actions are all sin." Proverbs 29:23 (NASB): "A man's pride will bring him low, but a humble spirit will obtain honor."

What does the term "haughty eyes" mean? Why does God hate this in a person? This term means a "proud look," reflective or someone who thinks more highly of himself than he should. A young man with haughty eyes, or a proud look, believes himself to be better than others. He is arrogant and selfish, caring only for himself and what *he* wants.

Humble is the opposite of *haughty*. *Humble* means "to be meek, kindhearted" and "to consider the needs of others before your own." Jesus was humble in every way, and He wants you to be like Him. Life is not all about you. Jesus teaches us to put the needs of others before our own, to be kind and helpful, and to be compassionate and loving. Jesus spent His time here on earth helping and healing others. He befriended the poor, the sinners, and the diseased. Jesus is the King of Kings, the Son of God, the Savior of the world, yet He humbled Himself and served others. Jesus humbled Himself enough to wash the dirty, smelly feet of his disciples. And even though He never did anything wrong, Jesus humbled Himself enough to die on a cross for you—a punishment normally reserved for only the worst crimes! He did all of these things to set an example for us to follow.

Jesus' friend and disciple, Peter, said this: "You younger men, likewise, be subject to your elders; and all of you, clothe yourselves with humility toward one another, for 'God is opposed to the proud, but gives grace to the humble.' Therefore humble yourselves under the mighty hand of God, that He may exalt you at the proper time, casting all your anxiety on Him, because He cares for you" (1 Peter 5:5 NASB). Peter says that if we humble ourselves and serve others in this life, we will be exalted or lifted up with praise in heaven.

References: John 13:5–15   Philippians 2:5–11   Proverbs 29:23
            1 Peter 5:5   James 4:10

Prayer: Dear God in heaven, my creator and my king, help me to humble myself in your sight and not be haughty. Help me to realize that I am nothing without you in my life. Please help me to put you first, others second, and myself last. In the name of Jesus Christ, the perfect example of humility and grace, I pray, amen.

Parents, Walk the Walk: Does your son see you acting proud or haughty when it comes to your home, car, clothes, or other earthly possessions? Are you a braggart? Is your heart full of pride because your child is smarter, more handsome, or "better" than the other children in your church or neighborhood? Remember that 1 Corinthians 10:12 (NASB) says, "Therefore let him who thinks he stands take heed that he does not fall."

Day 9 Liar, Liar, Pants on Fire!

Proverbs 6:16-19 (NASB): "There are six things which the LORD hates, yes, seven which are an abomination to Him: haughty eyes, a lying tongue, and hands that shed innocent blood, a heart that devises wicked plans, feet that run rapidly to evil, a false witness who utters lies, and one who spreads strife among brothers." Proverbs 12:22 (NASB): "Lying lips are an abomination to the Lord, but those who deal faithfully are His delight."

Why does God hate lying so much? Because lying and deceit come straight from the devil, the enemy of God. Jesus calls the devil, Satan, "the father of lies" (John 8:44 NASB) because he invented lying. We first read about Satan and his deception in the first book of the Bible, Genesis. He slithers up to Eve in the form of a snake and lies to her about the tree of the knowledge of good and evil. God put the tree in the garden of Eden and told Adam and Eve not to eat of it or they would die. The devil used deceit and lies to trick Eve into eating the fruit and then giving it to her husband to eat as well. Satan caused the first man and woman on earth to sin through the use of his lies. Because of their sin, Adam and Eve were thrown out of the garden and out of the presence of God.

The Bible tells us that Jesus is "the Way, the Truth and the Life" (John 14:6 NASB). All the words of Jesus are true and righteous and lead us to God. Since God and Satan are complete opposites, we know that the devil and his followers are full of lies, deceit, and all that is evil. Satan plants the seeds of lying and deceit into the hearts of men. It is up to each person to resist the urge to deceive or lie from time to time. If you are focusing on Jesus and God each day, then your heart is filled with honesty and goodness. If you are not thinking about the Lord, praying, and studying His word, then you leave your heart open to the devil and his demons to fill it with evil.

In the Book of Revelation, there are two separate lists of the kinds of people who will be found in hell when they die. These people are sinners—murderers, idol worshipers, and those who don't believe in Jesus. But what you may not know is that both lists also include "all liars" and "everyone who loves and practices lying." God tells us that people who do not try to tell the truth will end up in hell with murderers, idolaters, and all the other evil people who ever lived on the earth. Lying is very serious, and God hates it. It is simple; when you tell the truth, you are doing what God wants you to do; when you lie, you are doing what the devil wants you to do. Who will you follow?

References: Genesis 2:15–3:24   John 8:44   Revelation 21:8 and 22:15

Prayer: Dear holy Father, creator of all that is good and true and righteous, please help me to be honest and truthful in all that I say and do. Fill my heart and mind with honesty and goodness. Please help me resist when Satan tempts me to lie. In the name of Jesus Christ, your Son—the Way, the Truth, and the Life, amen.

Parents, Talk the Talk: Do you ever lie in front of your children? Maybe you do at times and do not even realize it. For example, someone who you do not want to speak with calls, so you tell your child to answer the phone and tell the caller that you're not there. Or have you possibly stretched the truth to avoid hurting someone's feelings? God does not categorize lies into "big" or "little" ones. To God, a lie is a lie. Even what *we* consider to be small "white lies" are serious to God and set a terrible example for our children.

Day 10: Hate No One

> Proverbs 6:16-19 (NASB): "There are six things which the LORD hates, yes, seven which are an abomination to Him: haughty eyes, a lying tongue, and hands that shed innocent blood, a heart that devises wicked plans, feet that run rapidly to evil, a false witness who utters lies, and one who spreads strife among brothers." I John 3:15 (NASB): "Everyone who hates his brother is a murderer; and you know that no murderer has eternal life abiding in him."

One of the seven things God hates is a person who sheds innocent blood—a murderer. While that is probably not something that you or anyone you know would ever be, you might struggle with another sin that God says is equal to murder—hate. Jesus' apostle and good friend, John, tells us that if you hate someone, you are just as bad as a murderer.

The opposite of hate is, of course, love. Jesus directly commands us to "love one another" three times (John 13:34, 15:12,17 NASB). Jesus even tells us that we must "love our enemies" (Matt.5:44 NASB). That can be extremely hard at times. But what kind of love is Jesus talking about? The word for *love* that Jesus uses in these commands is *agape*, which means to have regard for someone's welfare or to want the best for that person. Even if you don't like someone, you are supposed to have agape love for him or her. In the same way, God loves each one of us. He may not like the things we do from time to time, but He always loves us and wants what is best for us. In fact, God loves each of us so very much that He gave His only son, Jesus, to die on the cross so that we can have a chance to spend eternity in heaven with Him.

There are or will be people in your life who are mean, hateful, or even cruel to you. And while it is okay to hate the hurtful things they do, it is never okay to hate the person. What does Jesus tell us to do when we are being mistreated and find it hard to love or even like someone? He says,

"But I say unto you... Love your enemies, do good to those that hate you, bless those that curse you, pray for those who mistreat you." (Luke 6:27-28 NASB). We are supposed to care about and pray for the people who hurt us, even those we consider to be enemies. You can pray for them to change their hearts and stop hurting people. You should also pray for yourself—to always keep love and concern for others in your heart, even when it is hard to do.

References: 1 John 3:10–15   John 13:34 and 15:12,17
              Matthew 5:43–46   Luke 6:27–35   John 3:16

Prayer: Heavenly Father, thank you so much for loving me even when I do hurtful things to you or others. Please help me to love everyone and want what is best for them, as you do for me. Help me to resist the temptation to hate, and keep my heart full of love. Thank you for loving me so much that you sent your son to die for me. In His name, I pray, amen.

Parents, Talk the Talk: Is there someone in your life whom you hate? If so, your son can see it. Put all hatred out of your heart so that you can set the example of loving others for your child. The best way to stop hating someone is to forgive him for whatever wrong he has done to you, even if has not asked you to or never will.

Day 11: Don't Go Looking for Trouble!

Proverbs 6:16–19 (NASB): "There are six things which the LORD hates, yes, seven which are an abomination to Him: haughty eyes, a lying tongue, and hands that shed innocent blood, a heart that devises wicked plans, feet that run rapidly to evil, a false witness who utters lies, and one who spreads strife among brothers." Proverbs 6:12–15 (NLT): "Here is a description of worthless and wicked people: They are constant liars, signaling their true intentions to their friends by making signs with their eyes and feet and fingers. Their perverted hearts plot evil. They stir up trouble constantly. But they will be destroyed suddenly, broken beyond all hope of healing."

Do you know someone who is always stirring up or getting into trouble at home or at school? Does this person seem to enjoy the attention he or she receives for mischievous pranks or shocking language? Even though these people may seem popular among their peers, this is precisely the behavior that God hates.

It takes a lot of time and energy to devise evil plans or stir up trouble. God wants you to spend your time and energy doing good things and saying good words. Colossians 3:17 (NASB) tells us, "Whatever you do in word or deed, [do] all in the name of the Lord Jesus, giving thanks through Him to God the Father." Every deed we do and word we utter should be something that would bring honor to God, not shame.

The Bible tells us that our words and actions are a direct result of what is contained in our hearts. If a young man has an evil heart, then evil actions and vile speech will result. But if you have a pure heart, then good words and actions will naturally come forth. How can you keep your heart pure and righteous, as God would have you? You must fill your mind with uplifting thoughts. The apostle Paul gives us a list of things to think about:

21

"Finally, brothers, whatever is true, whatever is honorable, whatever is right, whatever is pure, whatever is lovely, whatever is of good repute, if there is any excellence and if anything worthy of praise, dwell on these things" (Philip.4:8 NASB). If you have filled your heart with good thoughts, it will be easy to fill your time and expend your energy doing good deeds, not stirring up trouble.

References: Colossians 3:17   Matthew 15:18–19   Mark 7:21–23
              Luke 6:43–45   Philippians 4:8–9   Proverbs 14:16–17, 22

Prayer: Holy God, please fill my heart, mind, and soul with your righteousness. Lord, help me to use my time doing and saying things that will bring honor to your glorious name. When I am tempted to join in with troublemakers, please give me the strength to stand firm and do what is right. In the name of your son and my Savior, Jesus, amen.

Parents, Walk the Walk: Do you ever stir up trouble among family or friends? Do you like to argue or enjoy controversy or scandal when it occurs in your church or neighborhood? Your son notices how you fill your time and what you discuss with other adults. Make sure that whatever you do, say, or become involved in would bring honor to God. Apply this litmus test: If it is not pure, lovely, of good repute, excellent, or praiseworthy, then don't go there.

Day 12: Don't Play the Blame Game

Proverbs 6:16-19 (NASB): "There are six things which the LORD hates, yes, seven which are an abomination to Him: haughty eyes, a lying tongue, and hands that shed innocent blood, a heart that devises wicked plans, feet that run rapidly to evil, a false witness who utters lies, and one who spreads strife among brothers." Proverbs 19:5 (NASB): "A false witness will not go unpunished, and he who tells lies will not escape."

You have probably seen a television show that depicts friends or perhaps brothers horsing around in the house, and subsequently one of them breaks something valuable, like a lamp or expensive vase. He knows that he broke a rule (like "no wrestling" or "no playing ball in the house") and will be punished. When the mom comes over and says, "Who did this?" they each point to the other and say, "He did it!" And, chances are, you have had a similar experience in your home or at school. In fact, this very thing happened to the first two people created by God—Adam and Eve. God told them they could eat from any tree in the garden of Eden except for one—the Tree of the Knowledge of Good and Evil. The devil approached Eve, disguised as a snake, and told her to eat some of the fruit from that tree because it looks good, tastes good, and will make her wise. So she eats it, even though God had told her very clearly not to. Then she gave it to her husband, Adam, and he ate some also. When God came and asked them if they had eaten the fruit, Eve said, "The serpent told me to, so I did." And then when God asked Adam, he said, "My wife gave it to me, so I ate it." Both Eve and Adam had disobeyed God. They were each guilty, having done exactly the one thing God had told them not to do. Afterward, instead of taking responsibility for their own actions and asking God to forgive them, they blamed someone else for what they had done.

We know that this concept of not blaming others is important to God.

In fact, "You shall not bear false witness ..." (Exodus 20:16 NASB) is one of the Ten Commandments that God issued to the people of Israel. But why does God hate this behavior so much? First of all, when you blame someone else for a sin or offense that you committed, you are lying. We already know that God hates "a lying tongue." Also, when you blame someone else for your mistake, or "bear false witness," that person, in turn, will receive the punishment that you rightfully deserve. God cannot tolerate injustice. His ways are upright, and His judgments are perfect. God expects you to take responsibility for your own actions as well as take any deserved punishment for doing wrong. When you commit a sin or break a rule, do the right thing: admit your mistake and accept the consequences you deserve.

References: Genesis 2 and 3   Proverbs 12:17
              Exodus 20:1–17 (The Ten Commandments)
              Deuteronomy 32:3–4

Prayer: Oh, God, you are holy and righteous. Your judgments are perfect. You see me as I am, with all my faults and sins. Please help me to admit when I make a mistake and accept my punishment with grace and maturity. Help me to learn from those mistakes and the consequences I deserve. In the name of Jesus I pray, amen.

Parents, Talk the Talk: Do you fault others for your problems at work or church or within your family? Do your sons hear you shift the blame for problems you really created yourself? When you make a serious mistake, own up to it and apologize to those you have hurt, especially if it is one of your children.

Day 13: Don't Gossip

Proverbs 6:16–19 (NASB): "There are six things which the LORD hates, yes, seven which are an abomination to Him: haughty eyes, a lying tongue, and hands that shed innocent blood, a heart that devises wicked plans, feet that run rapidly to evil, a false witness who utters lies, and one who spreads strife among brothers." Proverbs 20:19 (NASB): "He who goes about as a slanderer reveals secrets; therefore do not associate with a gossip."

Gossip, rumor, and *slander*—these three words are very closely connected, and God hates them all. But what do these words really mean? Well, when a friend tells you something about another person and you do not know if it is true, it is a rumor. The information this person passed on is gossip. And if the story was told to hurt someone's feelings or reputation, then that is slander. God hates gossip, rumors, and slander because they are deceitful and the only purpose they serve is to cause damage and heartache to another person.

If you have ever been the subject of gossip, then you know how it works. Someone at your school or in your neighborhood starts a rumor about you that is false in part or in whole. One person tells a group of people, who in turn tell others. Before long, the entire school or neighborhood has heard something about you that is not true. As you know, nothing good comes out of the process—only trouble. Gossip, rumors, and slander cause pain to the one being talked about, can break up friendships, and can ruin a person's reputation.

It can be very tempting to listen to a juicy piece of gossip about someone. You know it is coming when the conversation starts like this: "Did you hear about …?" Well, the Bible says, "The words of a gossip are like choice morsels; they go down to a man's inmost parts" (Prov.18:8 New International Version [NIV]). Gossip is like having candy or your favorite food sitting on a plate right in front of you—it is very hard to resist. If your friend begins talking to you or a group of people about someone else, you must stop the cycle of rumors. You must do what is right. Tell your friend that you do not want to hear gossip and change the subject or leave the room if it continues. Do not repeat anything you hear to anyone else.* The only way that gossip and rumors can be stopped is if people refuse to pass them on.

*There is only one exception to the gossip rule. If you hear talk about someone you know who is doing something dangerous to himself or others (such as drinking, taking drugs, hanging out with the wrong crowd, etc.), then you should tell your parents.

References: Proverbs 16:27–28   Proverbs 18:8 (NIV)

Prayer: Dear Lord, awesome God, please help me to listen to and repeat only good and truthful words. Please direct me away from gossip, rumors, and slander. Help me to stand up for what is right and stop the vicious cycle of gossip when I am faced with that dilemma. Thank you for your words of wisdom and grace. In the name of your holy and precious son, Jesus, amen.

Parents, Talk the Talk: Do you like to hear and/or repeat a juicy story about a neighbor, friend, or family member? Your son notices when you lower your voice in conversation so he won't hear what you are saying about another person. In fact, kids usually *do* hear the things we whisper about (even though they seem to tune us out the rest of the time we speak). Set the example for them to follow; don't listen to or repeat gossip.

Day 14: Obey Your Parents

Proverbs 6: 20 (NASB): "My son, observe the commandment of your father; and do not forsake the teaching of your mother."

Being a parent is a very hard job with many different responsibilities. One or possibly both of your parents work to provide money for your house, food, clothing, and other things you want and need. Your parents take care of your home, cook your food, wash your clothes, and perform other chores for you. Your parents help you with homework and school projects. They drive you to school, to church, and all around town to various activities and events. But the most important things they do for you are love you, protect you, and teach you to be a good person. A child, on the other hand, only has two main jobs or responsibilities in life: one is to go to school (and do your best), and the other is to obey your parents.

Why is it so important to obey your parents? The short answer is this: God and Jesus command you to. God specifically told His people, the Israelites, to "Honor your father and mother..." in the Ten Commandments (Exodus 20:12 NASB). *Honor* means to "respect and obey." In fact, under the law of Moses, a son could be stoned to death for being rebellious and disobeying his parents. While that harsh law is no longer in effect, the principle still applies to children today. The apostle Paul wrote to New Testament Christians, saying, "Children, obey your parents, in the Lord, for this is right" (Eph.6:1 NASB). Obeying your parents is the right thing to do. They deserve your love, respect, and honor. You show them that you love, respect, and honor them by listening to them and doing what they say.

Think about how you usually respond to your parents when they ask you to do something. Do you immediately stop what you are doing and obey, or do you question them or ignore their request? If you are not responding immediately and without complaint, then you are not giving your parents the honor and respect they deserve. Every time your parents ask you or tell you to do something, they are either trying to protect you or hoping to teach you something. You are their responsibility, so you must trust their judgment and believe that they have your best interests at heart when they make a request or issue an order. Obeying your parents is the smart thing to do. They know what is best for you. So remember this: when you obey your parents, you are also obeying God.

References: Exodus 20:12   Deuteronomy 5:16 and 21:18–21
             Ephesians 6:1–3

Prayer: Heavenly Father, thank you for giving me parents who love me and take care of me every day. Please help me to show my love, respect, and honor for them, and for you, by obeying their commands and yours. In the name of Jesus I pray, amen.

Parents, Walk the Walk: Do your children obey you? If not, do you wonder why? Are you disciplining them enough or possibly too much? Ephesians 6:4 (NASB) says, "Fathers, do not provoke your children to anger, but bring them up in the discipline and instruction of the Lord." Are you bringing them up according to the instructions of God?

Day 15: Make Your Parents Proud

Proverbs 10:1 (NASB): "A wise son makes a father glad, but a foolish son is a grief to his mother."

Have you ever done something in front of other people that made your mother and father hang their heads in shame? Maybe you threw a fit, argued with them, acted out for attention, were rude to an adult, or said words that were totally inappropriate. Or there may have been times when you were not with your parents and you did something that you knew they would be ashamed of—if they ever found out.

When you act foolishly and do things that are shameful, you hurt yourself, your parents, and Jesus. Believers in Christ are expected to behave differently than people of the world. This applies to kids just as much as adults. In fact, the Bible says that Christians are to be a "peculiar" people. This does not mean you are supposed to be weird or strange; it means you are to be set apart and different. When the kids around you are using bad language, treating others unkindly, and being disrespectful to their parents and other adults, you are supposed to be different from them and do the right thing. You should bring honor to Jesus and your parents through your actions, not shame.

The apostle Paul told his young friend Timothy, "Don't let anyone look down on you because you are young, but set an example for the believers in speech, in life, in love, in faith and in purity." (I Tim.4:12 NIV) The easiest way to be an example of good behavior in front of others is to think before you do or say something. If you are not sure about a situation, ask yourself this question: "Would this bring honor to me, my parents, and my Savior—or shame?" Your parents and your God deserve your best behavior, not your worst.

All parents want to be proud of their children. Our heavenly Father wants to be proud of His children as well. Be wise and make your earthly parents, as well as your heavenly Father, proud of you in all you do and say.

References: 1 Peter 2:9   1 Timothy 4:12   Proverbs 17:25

Prayer: Great and mighty God, I thank you for sending your Son, Jesus, to be my Savior. I am so grateful that Jesus was not ashamed to die for my sins. Please help me to act in a way that does not shame you, Jesus, or my parents. Guide me down paths of righteousness and help me to set a good example for others to follow. In the name of Jesus Christ I pray, amen.

Parents, Walk the Walk: Shame and embarrassment are a two-way street. Have you ever done or said something in front of your child or his friends that you were ashamed of later? We set the stage for our children's behavior. If we do things to embarrass our sons, chances are that we will get the same treatment in return.

Day 16: Don't Be Lazy

Proverbs 10:5 (NASB): "He who gathers in summer is a son who acts wisely, but he who sleeps in harvest is a son who acts shamefully."

Back in the days of King Solomon, sons were expected to work. They helped plant and harvest crops; they helped hunt for meat or tend to their families' flocks of sheep or goats; and they learned their fathers' trades and studied the law of God. If a child was lazy and did not do his fair share of the work, the whole family would suffer. Today, most boys are not required to actually hunt, work in a field, or shepherd a flock for their families' food. However, being lazy is not pleasing to God, so you should still work to help out your family and for yourself.

There are many jobs that need to be done around your house: taking out the trash, keeping your room neat and clean, pulling weeds, raking the yard, folding and putting away your clean clothes, feeding and caring for your pet—the list goes on and on. If you are lazy and don't help with these or other chores at your home, then another family member has to do your work.

You also have the responsibility of working hard and doing your best in school. If you are lazy and do not study for tests or complete your homework, you are not learning the things you should know and are only hurting yourself. Schoolwork, like chores at home, is usually not considered "fun," but it is necessary. King Solomon said, "Whatever your hand finds to do, do it with all your might, for in the grave, where you are going, there is neither working nor planning nor knowledge nor wisdom" (Ecclesiastes 9:10 NIV). He is telling you to take pride in all the work that you do while you are living here on earth, whether it is "fun" or not. Whatever you do, do your best.

In addition to home and school, there is also work to be done for the

Lord. Attending services, studying the Bible, telling others about Jesus, and helping those in need are even more important jobs than those at home or at school. The apostle Paul tells Christians, "Never be lazy in your work, but serve the Lord enthusiastically" (Romans 12:11 NLT). We should work just as hard for the Lord as we do at home for our parents and for our teachers at school.

The next time your parents ask you to do a chore, your teacher gives an assignment, or you are asked to do a job at church, respond eagerly and do the task to the best of your ability. When you are finished, you should feel a sense of accomplishment and pride.

References: Ecclesiastes 9:10 (NIV)   Romans 12:11(NLT)
              Proverbs 6:6–11

Prayer: Awesome and mighty God, you worked hard to create this beautiful world and everything in it. Help me to resist the temptation to be lazy. Please give me strength to please you by being a hard worker at home, at school, and in my church. Instill in me a sense of pride in all that I do and help me to perform all my jobs to the best of my abilities. In Jesus' name, amen.

Parents, Walk the Walk: Do you complain about your job or chores at home? Your son will be more enthusiastic about his responsibilities if he sees you doing your work with pride and pleasure. But even more importantly, does your son see you working for Jesus? Do you get up each Sunday morning to take your son to worship? Are you involved and working in the church, or do you just go to service and do nothing more? Read Proverbs 6:6–11 with your son and talk to him about the importance and rewards of hard work.

Day 17: Be a Good Listener

Proverbs 10: 19-20 (NASB): "When there are many words, transgression is unavoidable, but he who restrains his lips is wise."

Is it hard for you to be quiet and listen to someone else talk about something he or she has done, tell a joke or story, or explain a situation; do you want to butt in and give your opinion, tell your story, or give your explanation instead of letting the other person speak? Do your parents, teachers, or other adults often have to tell you to be quiet? If so, then you talk too much. The more you talk, the higher your chances are of saying the wrong thing, missing out on important information, or annoying and alienating the people around you.

If you talk all the time, nonstop, you cannot be a good listener, a good friend, a successful student, or an attentive and obedient child. If you are talking when your teacher or parent is trying to say something important, then you cannot follow his or her directions. If you are talking when your friend is attempting to speak, you are annoying and being rude to your friend. Other people like to be listened to and feel that what they say matters to you. The Bible tells us that we should be "quick to hear, slow to speak." (James 1:19 NASB) That means be quiet and listen, and then think about what you want to say before it comes out of your mouth.

Sometimes it is hard to be quiet and not speak, especially if you are a friendly and outgoing person. James, the brother of Jesus, tells us in his book of the Bible that the tongue, while small, is the most powerful part of the body. He compares the tongue to the rudder of a huge ship, which is small but able to turn the ship and control its direction. You should control your tongue, not let your tongue control you.

King Solomon tells us, "A word fitly spoken is like apples of gold in pictures of silver" (Prov. 25:11 KJV). What a beautiful picture that conjures in our minds. He is telling us with these descriptive words that our speech should be beautiful and pleasing to those who hear it. We should try to never say anything ugly, crude, rude, offensive, harsh, or insulting. Jesus listens to everything we say and every conversation we engage in. He tells us very clearly that on the day of judgment, we will give an account to God of every word we have ever spoken. Don't talk so much that your words get you into trouble.

References: James 3:1–12   Colossians 4:6   1 Timothy 6:20a
                  Proverbs 25:11   Matthew 12:34–37

Prayer: Holy Father, hallowed is your name. Thank you for creating the gifts of hearing and speech and for blessing me with both. Touch my mind, ears, and mouth; and produce in me the desire to listen to others, the self-control to be quiet, and the wisdom to speak the proper words at the proper time. May everything I say bring glory and honor to you. In the name of Jesus Christ I pray, amen.

Parents, Talk the Talk: Does your son's "gift of gab" come naturally? Did he inherit that trait from you? If so, help your son turn it into an honorable characteristic, not a character flaw. Read James 3: 1-12 with your son and talk to him about the power of the tongue. James compares the tongue not only to the rudder of a ship but also to a forest fire started by the smallest match. These are powerful illustrations that can teach children (and parents) the importance of taming the tongue.

Day 18: Be Trustworthy

Proverbs 11:13 (NASB): "He who goes about as a talebearer reveals secrets, but he who is trustworthy conceals a matter."

One of the easiest and best ways to be a good friend is to keep a secret. Has anyone ever told you something very private and asked you to promise not to tell? Did you keep your word? If not, then you betrayed your friend's trust. That friend, and all the others you told, can no longer trust you. When you are trustworthy and keep your word to a friend, you show your friend that you care about him or her and that you are loyal.

Trust is important to your parents as well. When you tell your parents that you will do something they have asked of you and then don't, you are not being dependable or truthful. If you do things when your parents are not around that you know they would disapprove of, you not only dishonor them but also betray their trust. If you want to be treated as a mature young man, then you must give your parents a reason to trust you by obeying them every time, even when they are not around. Trust is earned, not given.

You certainly want your friends and parents to be able to trust you, but what about your heavenly Father and His Son, Jesus? We know that they are trustworthy and will keep all the promises laid out for us in the Bible. Can Jesus trust you to always follow Him and keep His commandments? If you have made a commitment to being His faithful disciple, then you must keep your word to the Lord and do His will. Be dependable in your worship attendance and in your daily Bible study. Be trustworthy in all that you say and do with your friends, your parents, and everyone you meet. By doing so, you will earn their respect and the praise of your heavenly Father.

References: Proverbs 20:19   Proverbs 28:20 (NLT)

Prayer: Dear Lord of heaven and earth, thank you for keeping all your promises to me. Help me to be honest, truthful, and trustworthy in all my dealings with friends and family and especially in my walk with you, God. Please give me an honest and loyal heart so that others will trust me. In your perfect Son Jesus' name I pray, amen.

Parents, Walk the Walk: Do you keep your word to your son? Do you keep the secrets and personal details he shares with you confidential? Never betray your son's trust or embarrass him by revealing his secrets or personal information to others. Do you make promises to him and then not follow through? If you tell him you will do something, make every effort to do it. By keeping your word to your children, you will teach them trust, responsibility, and dependability.

Day 19: Cheaters Never Prosper

Proverbs 11:1 (NLT): "The Lord hates cheating, but he delights in honesty."

Every person has been tempted to cheat at one time or another. It could be during an important test at school, a sporting event, or even a silly game of checkers. We all like to win; however, God *hates* cheating. It is dishonest. When you cheat, not only do you lose favor in God's eyes; you also lose your integrity and your own self-respect–and, if you are caught, the respect of others as well.

If you cheat in school, it means that you did not actually learn the material you needed to know in order to make the grade you desired. Not knowing that important information will only hinder your ability to learn new concepts. If you cheat in sports by not following the rules, then you will have gained an unfair advantage over your opponent. What joy is there in beating someone through trickery? If you cheat on your girlfriend, not only will she have hurt feelings, but the other girls you know will never trust you, and your reputation will be tarnished. In all these situations, cheating does not gain you any reward; it only hurts you and others.

The writer of Luke tells us, "Unless you are faithful in small matters, you won't be faithful in large ones. If you cheat even a little, you won't be honest with greater responsibilities." (Luke 16:10 NLT) This means that when you yield to the temptation to cheat, you are falling into a trap. You may start out cheating on something small and seemingly insignificant, like that silly game of checkers. From that point on, you could be tempted to continue cheating in more important areas of life. People who cheat to win do not actually win at all. The score may say they are victorious, but they are really losers in what matters most—their standing with God. Succeed in everything you do through honesty, hard work, and perseverance, not cheating, lies, and deceit.

References:　Luke 16:10–12　　Proverbs 10:9

Prayer: Thank you, dear Lord, for my mind and my abilities. Please help me to use the talents you have given me to succeed in life. Remove from me the temptation to win or to get ahead of others through cheating, lies, and deceit. Lead me down the path of righteousness following your Son, Jesus, and prick my conscience when I stray. In His name I pray, amen.

Parents, Walk the Walk: Do you ever cheat your friends such as while playing cards; your government such as on your taxes; your God by not giving all you could in your weekly contribution to your church; or in any other situation? Proverbs 28:6 says it is "Better to be poor and honest than to be dishonest and rich." (NLT) To God, cheating is in the same category as lying and stealing. The Israelites were commanded, "Do not steal; do not cheat one another, do not lie." (Leviticus 19:11 NLT). Make sure your son never sees you cheat.

Day 20: Don't Worry, Be Happy

Proverbs 12:25 (NLT): "Worry weighs a person down; an encouraging word cheers a person up."

There are a lot of things in this world that a young man can worry about—school and grades; sports and other extracurricular activities; problems with girls, friends, or family. The older you get, even more things will cause you to be anxious: your job, taxes, your children, the economy, politics—the list goes on and on. However, God loves you, cares for you, and does not want you to spend all your time worrying about life here on earth.

Jesus tells His followers in Matthew 6:25–34 (NLT): "So I tell you, don't worry about everyday life—whether you have enough food, drink, and clothes. Doesn't life consist of more than food and clothing? Look at the birds. They don't need to plant or harvest or put food in barns because your heavenly Father feeds them. And you are far more valuable to him than they are. Can all your worries add a single moment to your life? Of course not. And why worry about your clothes? Look at the lilies and how they grow. They don't work or make their clothing, yet Solomon in all his glory was not dressed as beautifully as they are. And if God cares so wonderfully for flowers that are here today and gone tomorrow, won't he more surely care for you? You have so little faith! So don't worry about having enough food or drink or clothing. Why be like the pagans who are so deeply concerned about these things? Your heavenly Father already knows all your needs, and he will give you all you need from day to day if you live for him and make the Kingdom of God your primary concern. So don't worry about tomorrow, for tomorrow will bring its own worries. Today's trouble is enough for today."

Jesus is not telling us that we should not *care* about the daily issues we face in life. Your parents do have to work to provide the things you need—they will not just magically appear—and you still have to study for tests, practice your sport, handle problems at school or at home, and deal with difficult people or circumstances from time to time. What Jesus is saying is that if we work hard and do our best; trust in God; and put Jesus, His word, and His church first in our lives, then He will make sure we are taken care of. When you are worried about something, go to your heavenly Father in prayer. He knows everything that is going on in your life and knows what you need to handle the situation. The apostle Paul tells us, "Don't worry about anything; instead, pray about everything. Tell God what you need, and thank him for all he has done. Then you will experience God's peace, which exceeds anything we can understand. His peace will guard your hearts and minds as you live in Christ Jesus." (Phil. 4:6-7 NLT)

References: Matthew 6:25–34   Matthew 11:28–30
              Philippians 4:6–7(NLT)

Prayer: Eternal God and Father of all who are redeemed by the blood of your Son, I know that you take care of your children. Please give me your peace and help me to cease worrying. Help me to lean on you, pray to you when I have a problem, and trust you to work all things for my good. In the name of Jesus, amen.

Parents, Walk the Walk: It is almost impossible as an adult and a parent to not worry about your children or the responsibilities of life. However, your son needs to know that you place your faith and trust in God. Pray to God about every care and burden you may carry and give them over to the Lord. Then teach your son to pray anytime he has a concern, no matter how small, and ask for God's guidance and comfort.

Day 21: Walk with the Wise

Proverbs 13:20 (NASB): "He who walks with wise men will be wise, but the companion of fools will suffer harm."

Everyone is faced with making difficult decisions from time to time, including you. Sometimes you may feel overwhelmed and unsure of what you should do when a problem arises. When something is bothering you, who do you turn to for advice? If you have an issue at school, church, or home that needs to be resolved, talking to friends can help. However, when faced with important, life-changing dilemmas, you should seek the advice of older and wiser companions.

Unfortunately, King Solomon's own son did not heed his father's advice to "walk with wise men." After Solomon's death, his son Rehoboam became king over the twelve tribes of Israel, a mighty and wealthy nation. During his forty-year reign, Solomon had highly taxed and overworked the people while building the glorious temple of God, and they were tired of it. Israel sent a representative, Jeroboam, to Rehoboam to ask him to lighten the load of the people. Jeroboam assured the new king that if he made their lives easier, the people would faithfully serve him. Rehoboam first sought the counsel of the elders who had served his father, Solomon. Their advice was to "grant them [the peoples] their petition and speak good words to them, then, they will be your servants forever." (I Kings 12:7b NASB)) Rehoboam then went to the young men who had grown up with him and asked their opinion. His younger, inexperienced friends told him he should add to the heavy burdens already imposed by Solomon and rule the people even more severely. Rehoboam took the advice of his young friends, instead of the wiser, older men. When the people of Israel heard Rehoboam's response, they rebelled and divided the kingdom. Ten of the tribes chose Jeroboam to be their king, leaving Rehoboam with only two tribes, a mere fraction of the once mighty nation, to rule. Rehoboam made a grave mistake by choosing the wrong advice.

Your parents, grandparents, elders, deacons, and teachers at church are all older, wiser people who can give you valuable counsel. Why? Well, because, at some time in their lives, they have dealt with the same problems, questions, or situations that you are facing as a young man. You can learn from their experiences, their mistakes, their successes, and even their failures. Don't be a Rehoboam. Instead, walk with the wise and seek their advice.

Reference: 1 Kings 12: 1–24   Proverbs 12:15 (NLT)

Prayer: Heavenly Father, grant me the wisdom to respect my elders and seek their guidance when I face challenges and choices that I don't know how to handle. I know that you have placed wise, older people in my life for this very purpose. Please allow me to follow their counsel and do everything in accordance with your will for my life. In Jesus' name I pray, amen.

Parents, Talk the Talk: Do you encourage your son to come to you with his concerns, dilemmas, and important choices in life? Children often have a hard time believing that their parents lived through the same types of problems they are facing. Spend time talking about all the issues your son struggles with. Even though you grew up in a different era, the problems young people face never really change. Tell him how you handled similar situations, and if you made a mistake, tell him so that he can learn from it instead of repeating it.

Day 22: Don't Believe Everything You Hear (See or Read)

Proverbs 14:15(NASB): "The naïve believes everything, but the sensible man considers his steps."

If you look up the word *naive* in the dictionary, you will find this definition: "lacking in worldly wisdom or informed judgment." It also means "gullible," "easily tricked," and "unsuspecting." People who are naive believe anything they see, hear, or read or will fall for any prank, scam, or hoax that they encounter. You are naive about many things simply because you have not had all of the life experiences that your parents and other adults have. However, just because you are young, and yes, naive in certain areas, doesn't mean you are stupid or unable to make logical and intelligent choices.

The world is full of good, honest, innocent, and beautiful things. It is also filled with lies, sin, and danger. How do you sort the righteous from the evil? How do you know what is upright and true and not lies or deceit? The best way to know more about a subject is to study it before you develop an opinion. Reading or seeing something on the Internet or television or in a magazine or newspaper does not make it completely accurate or even true at all. Many individuals will write outrageous or shocking stories just for attention or profits. Before you repeat a story as a fact, do research and make sure that you know it is legitimate, true, and worth repeating.

You may have heard the phrase, "If it seems too good to be true, it probably is." Many people in the world enjoy playing pranks and hoaxes or even make their living by scamming others. If you are presented with a situation in which someone wants to give you something of value for little or nothing in return, watch out! It could be a prank, scam, or hoax. The best way to thwart a scheme is to use your common sense and your gut feelings. If you are in a circumstance in which something "just doesn't feel right," then get out of it immediately.

The verse above says that the naive believe everything but that a sensible man will consider his steps. This means that you need to be careful and consider your options before you believe something or act on something that you are unsure of. King Solomon says, "The naive inherit foolishness, but the sensible are crowned with knowledge." (Prov.14:18 NASB) When in doubt, pray first and ask the Lord to guide your way. Then, "crown yourself with knowledge"—do the research necessary to determine the sensible course of action.

References: Proverbs 14:18   Proverbs 22:3   Proverbs 23:23
                      Proverbs 1:32

Prayer: How great You are, God Almighty. Thank you for blessing me with intelligence and common sense. Help me to use these tools to discern between truth and lies. Please keep me safe from those who would seek to harm me through deceit, pranks, or other mischief. In the name of Jesus I pray, amen.

Parents, Walk the Walk: One of the best ways you can prepare your son for adulthood is to teach him how not to be gullible. Monitor what he is reading, hearing on the radio, and seeing on television and, especially, the Internet. Show him how to use urban legend sites like Snopes.com to research stories he is exposed to. He needs to know that things like chain letters and other hoaxes are not truthful and are certainly not appropriate to share with others.

Day 23: You Cannot Hide from God

Proverbs 15:3 (NASB): "The eyes of the Lord are in every place, watching the evil and the good."

Have you ever done something wrong that no one witnessed, so you got away with it and were not punished? Well, guess what. Someone did see you—God. God sees everything you do, even in secret. God is omniscient, which means that He is all-seeing and all-knowing. God is also omnipotent, which means that He is all-powerful, and God is omnipresent, which means that He has always existed in every place and always will. God knows every move you make, every word you say, and even every thought you think.

Jesus explains this to His disciples in Matthew 10. He encourages them to not be afraid of those who will seek to kill them because God, their heavenly Father, watches over them at all times. Jesus says, "Don't be afraid of those who want to kill you. They can only kill your body; they cannot touch your soul. Fear only God, who can destroy both soul and body in hell. Not even a sparrow, worth only half a penny, can fall to the ground without your Father knowing it. And the very hairs on your head are all numbered. So don't be afraid; you are more valuable to him than a whole flock of sparrows." (Matt. 10:28-31 NLT) Jesus tells them that God knows *everything* that happens in our world, even when a tiny sparrow falls to the ground. Of course the disciples were, and you are, much more important to God than a bird. God made you and He knows you personally. He follows every detail of your life. He is always watching you and loving you. In fact, God even knows exactly how many hairs you have on your head!

Because your heavenly Father knows everything about you, it is so important to live your life as if you are being watched at all times. You are! You are never really alone. God is there, and He sees all that you do, hears all that you say, and knows every intent of your heart. Galatians 6:7 tells us, "Do not be deceived, God is not mocked; for whatever a man sows, this he will also reap." In this verse, Paul is telling you not to kid yourself; you cannot fool God. Not only that, but you will eventually face the consequences of all the wrong you do, even things you thought you got away with. You may pull the wool over your parents' or teachers' eyes from time to time, but you can never hide from or trick God.

References: Matthew 10:28–31   Psalm 94:9–11   Hebrews 4:13

Prayer: Oh, God, you are omnipotent, omniscient, and omnipresent! Even so, I know that I am important to you. Thank you for watching over me day and night. You know my every deed, word, and thought. Help me to remember that you see when I am tempted to do wrong. Thank you for being interested in every minute detail of my life and for loving me even when I sin against you or my parents. Please forgive me for all my past transgressions, even those done in secret. In the name of your perfect Son, Jesus, amen.

Parents, Talk the Talk: When you reprimand your son for misbehaving or disobeying you, remind him that he has disappointed not only you but also God. Read the beautiful words of David in Psalms 139 with your son. Talk to him about God's omniscience and make sure your child thinks periodically about how God watches over him, knows his deeds and the thoughts of his heart; it is excellent motivation for doing what is right.

Day 24: Never Make Fun of People

Proverbs 17:5 (NASB): "He who mocks the poor taunts his Maker; he who rejoices at calamity will not go unpunished."

The Book of Genesis tells us that the first human being, Adam, was created "in the image of God." All human beings are created by God and in His image. Because of this special bond we share with God, we should treat all fellow human beings with respect. When someone makes fun of another person, God takes it personally. He will not tolerate the mocking or taunting of His creation. In fact, He gives very specific instructions about how to treat people who are often targeted for abuse.

In Leviticus19:14 (NLT), God told the children of Israel, "Show your fear of God by treating the deaf with respect and by not taking advantage of the blind." You should never, ever make fun of a person who has any type of physical or mental handicap. It is cruel. People who are blind, are deaf, were born with Down syndrome, are missing a limb, are overweight, or have any type of mental or bodily abnormality were all made by God and are special to God. They are loved by God just as much as you are. People cannot help that they were born with a deformity or that they have a physical disability related to an accident or an illness. People with disabilities have feelings and should always be treated with kindness and respect. God demands it!

In Leviticus 19:32 (NLT), God also commanded his people, "Show your fear of God by standing up in the presence of elderly people and showing respect for the aged." Hopefully, you already show respect for those older than yourself when you interact with your parents, grandparents, teachers, and coaches. But *all* elderly persons deserve your respect, even complete strangers and the cranky old man who lives on your street. You should never laugh at, make fun of, or try to harm an elderly person. One day, if you are fortunate enough to live a long life, you will be old too, and you will appreciate it when a young person is kind and treats you with the honor and respect you deserve.

Proverbs 22:2 (NASB) says, "The rich and the poor have a common bond, The Lord is the maker of them all." You are rich compared to most of the people in the world. You have shelter, food to eat, clothes to wear, and many other material blessings. When you see a person who is homeless, someone driving a run-down car, or a kid who does not dress as nicely as you, do not mock or taunt him or her. Those who are less fortunate need your prayers and support, not teasing or disrespect. Jesus commands all "rich" Christians to share their blessings and distribute them to those in need. Be thankful that you have been given so much and eager to help anyone you encounter who is "poor" compared to you.

References: Genesis 1: 26–28   1 Peter 2:17   1 Timothy 6:17–18

Prayer: Dear God, creator of all life, thank you for blessing me physically in countless ways. I know that you created all human beings in your image and that we are all "wonderfully" made by You. I also know that every soul is precious to you and that you gave your Son to die for the whole world. Please help me treat all people, regardless of physical ability, appearance, age, or station in life, with respect and kindness. In Jesus' name, amen.

Parents, Talk the Talk: Do you make negative comments when an older person is driving slowly in front of you or when you see a homeless person begging for money, or do you make off-colored remarks about the mentally challenged or minority groups? Even if you are just kidding around, your son will think it is okay to laugh at or ridicule others who are different.

Day 25: Set a Good Example
for Others to Follow

Proverbs 20:11 (NASB): "It is by his deeds that a lad distinguishes himself, if his conduct is pure and right."

In Matthew 5:16 (NASB), Jesus said, "Let your light shine before men in such a way that they may see your good works, and glorify your Father who is in heaven." No matter what you are doing, if other people are around, they are watching you. Perfect strangers, as well as your friends, should always be able to tell that you are a Christian by your words and actions. Everything you do and say in front of others should be a direct reflection of your relationship with Jesus. You must be a shining "light" for those who are living in sin and darkness. When you set a good example, your light will lead others down the right path—to Jesus.

The apostle Paul told his young friend Timothy, "Don't let anyone look down on you because you are young, but set an example for the believers in speech, in life, in love, in faith and in purity." (I Tim. 4:12 NIV) Even your Christian friends, fellow "believers," need encouragement at times. There are so many temptations for young people that it is important that you help your Christian friends stay focused on living for Jesus. Behaving like a Christian when you are around your fellow believers is just as important as behaving like a Christian in front of strangers or non- believing friends.

Jesus was sinless, and He set the perfect example for us. He did all things for the glory of His Father in heaven. And while He does not expect you to be perfect, He does expect you to do your best to follow in His steps, doing all things for the glory of God and setting a good example for all those around you. Jesus told His disciples, "I have given you an example to follow. Do as I have done to you" (John 13:15 NLT).

The proverb above rightly says that your deeds will be what distinguishes you from other people. When you perform deeds that are good and your "conduct is pure and right," then you are letting your light shine for Jesus. If you engage in sinful behavior instead, then you are following the lead of the devil and taking others down that dark path with you. The apostle Paul also instructed his friend Titus to "urge the young men to be self controlled ... to be an example of good deeds, with purity in doctrine, dignified, sound in speech which is beyond reproach" (Titus 2:6-8 NASB). If you will follow Jesus' perfect example in all things, doing everything to glorify God, then you and your light will lead those around you down paths of righteousness.

References: 1 Timothy 4:12   John 13:15   1 Peter 2:21–24
            Ephesians 5:1–4   Titus 2:6–8

Prayer: Holy Father, God of heaven and earth, thank you for sending your Son to be the perfect example for me to follow. Help me to think about everything I do and say before I act. Let me set a good example for others to follow wherever I may be. Guide me down your path of righteousness and allow me to lead others to you. In Jesus' name I pray, amen.

Parents, Walk the Walk: Your job as a parent is to always set the best possible example for your children to follow. Do you reflect the light of Jesus to your son, friends, family members, and strangers? Do they "see your good works and glorify your Father in heaven"? If you follow Jesus' example in all you say and do, then you will naturally lead your children and others to Christ.

Day 26: Do Not Seek Revenge

Proverbs 20:22 (NASB): "Do not say, 'I will repay evil;' wait for the Lord and He will save you."

There have been, or will be, times in your life when someone will truly hurt you—perhaps accidentally but maybe even on purpose. Occasionally, you will encounter hateful people at school or in your neighborhood who enjoy insulting and bullying others. Sometimes, people in your own family will do things that are hurtful. When this happens, the natural reaction to being harmed, either physically or emotionally, is to fight back, to hurt them in return. But this is not God's will for those who follow Him.

God told His chosen people, the Israelites, in Leviticus 19:18 (NLT), "Never seek revenge or bear a grudge against anyone, but love your neighbor as yourself. I am the Lord." It is hard to feel love for someone who has just hurt you, but it is commanded by God. Not only did God command this of the Israelites who followed the law of Moses, He also commands it of you and all Christians today. Romans 12:17–19 (NASB) says, "Never pay back evil for evil to anyone. Respect what is right in the sight of all men. If possible, so far as it depends on you, be at peace with all men. Never take your own revenge, beloved, but leave room for the wrath [of God,] for it is written, 'Vengeance is mine, I will repay,' says the Lord."

You have already learned that God sees and knows everything that happens to you. He knows when you have been wronged, and He knows the heart of the person responsible. God knows the crime against you and the best punishment for it. When you exact revenge against someone who has hurt you, you are doing God's work. You are not supposed to take matters into your own hands but to wait on the Lord; He will repay according to His plan and in His time. When you have been harmed by someone, your responsibility is to, first, pray for the person who hurt you, that he or she will have a changed heart and seek to make it right; second, forgive the person regardless of whether he or she asks for forgiveness; and third, trust God to work it all out for your good. God said, "Vengeance is mine, I will repay," and we must trust His judgment to repay those who are evil and harm others. Don't think you can do that job better than God.

References: Proverbs 24:29   Isaiah 35:4   Romans 8:28

Prayer: Heavenly Father, thank you for being a God of mercy and justice. Your word says that I must forgive others to receive forgiveness from you. Please forgive me for all the wrongs I have done to others, and help me to forgive those who harm me by mistake or on purpose. Help me to resist the temptation to seek revenge and pay back hurt for hurt. I trust you and your judgments because I know that you work all things together for my good. In the name of your Son, Jesus, I pray, amen.

Parents, Talk the Talk: Read the story of Cain and Abel from Genesis, Chapter 4:1-14, with your son. Discuss with him how harmful seeking and exacting revenge can be. Do you hold a grudge when someone hurts you? Do you get even? God will not forgive your trespasses unless you forgive those who trespass against you.

Day 27: "Kill Them with Kindness"

Proverbs 25:21–22 (NASB): "If your enemy is hungry, give him food to eat; and if he is thirsty, give him water to drink. For you will heap burning coals on his head, and the Lord will reward you."

When you think of an enemy, many different thoughts come to mind. There are enemies of our country, terrorists who want to harm us and take away our freedom; there are famous villains in movies you watch and books you read; and perhaps you may even have one or more of your own personal foes. Words that naturally come to mind when you consider an enemy are *attack, fight,* and *retaliate.* Wars, battles, duels, and fistfights have all erupted as a result of this thought process for thousands of years. While our armed forces will handle the enemies of the United States and superheroes like Batman and Superman will defeat their nemeses in the comic books or cartoons, God and Jesus have given you a wiser, more strategic plan for handling your own personal adversaries.

Jesus tells us in Matthew 5:44-45 (NASB), "But I say to you, love your enemies and pray for those who persecute you, so that you may be sons of your Father who is in heaven; for He causes His sun to rise on [the] evil and [the] good, and sends rain on [the] righteous and [the] unrighteous." The word *love* in this passage means to "care about; want what is best for." Jesus commands you to care about and want what is best for everyone, including your enemy, just as He does. Jesus died for all people—even mean, violent, or evil people—and He wants everyone to know Him and be saved. If you want to follow Jesus, you must love all people and treat them the way you want to be treated, even if they do not do the same in return and even if it is not easy to do.

God's ways are better than man's. His plan for how to defend yourself against an enemy is probably the opposite of your normal reaction. Instead of returning someone's abuse with an insulting remark or other deed of retaliation, God says to use kindness as your weapon of choice. Think of how taken aback that person would be if your response to his or her mean words or actions was one of love and kindness in return. If you are continually nice to someone who is ugly to you, it will kill that person's mean spirit. Bullies thrive on having the upper hand; they want to control you, upset you, and incite a fight. But if you respond with the opposite and totally unexpected reaction, you spoil their fun and they no longer have any reason to pick on you. The next time someone is hateful to you, don't reciprocate with anger and more hate; instead, "kill them with kindness."

References: Matthew 5:38–48   John 3:16   Romans 12:17–21

Prayer: Merciful God, thank you for loving all people that you have created. Thank you for offering your grace to all who will accept Jesus and respond to your plan of salvation. Please help me to care about and treat others the way you want me to. Help me to respond to insults and abuse with kindness, and forgive me when I don't. In the name of Jesus, my Savior and friend, I pray, amen.

Parents, Talk the Talk: Read the entire passage of Matthew 5:38–48 to your son. Talk to him about how Jesus wants us to handle minor offenses by turning the other cheek and how He wants us to pray for and care about everyone—even our enemies.

Day 28: Control Yourself

Proverbs 25:28 (NLT): "A person without self-control is as defenseless as a city with broken-down walls."

Back in Bible times, large and important cities were protected by walls. A high, strong wall would keep out enemies and those seeking to attack and pillage. If the enemy breached and broke down the wall, they were able to invade and often times defeat and take over the city. King Solomon, who knew the importance of the wall surrounding his city, Jerusalem, tells us that self-control serves as our wall against sin to help us keep out our number-one enemy–the devil.

You will be tempted many times in your life to go along with a friend or a crowd that is not doing what is right. You may be asked to smoke, drink alcohol, or try some kind of drug; you might be in a car that is going too fast or on the way to a party where the wrong crowd of people will be; you may be involved with a girlfriend who wants to do inappropriate things; or you may be in many other scenarios in which you will have to choose whether or not to stand up and do the right thing. Self-control is the characteristic you must develop in order to resist these and other temptations that you are certain to face.

The apostle Peter tells us, "Be self-controlled and alert. Your enemy, the devil, prowls like a roaring lion looking for someone to devour." (1 Peter 5:8 NIV) Even though you do not see an actual lion stalking you as prey, Satan is real, is roaming the earth, and is active in every temptation that comes your way. He wants to breach your wall, invade your heart, and take over your life. He wants you to serve him instead of God.

How do you develop the self-control that is necessary to keep the devil out? You must submit to God by giving your mind, heart, and soul to the Lord Jesus Christ. In the Book of James, Jesus' brother says, "Submit therefore to God. Resist the devil and he will flee from you. "(James 4:7 NASB) If you submit your heart to Jesus, follow His plan of salvation, live for Him each day, and do His commandments, then you will acquire the strength of will and self-control needed to resist the devil and the temptations that he will cast your way. As your faith and devotion to God grow, your wall against the forces of evil will also grow stronger and more secure.

References: 1 Peter 5:8–9 (NIV)   James 4:7   Romans 12:21

Prayer: My Lord and my God, help me to fully submit my life, my will, and my heart to you, your Son, and your service. I know that through your might and power, I can make the walls of my heart strong enough to withstand any temptation. Help me to read and use your Word to build my character and self-control each day. In Jesus' name I pray, amen.

Parents, Talk the Talk: One of the best ways to arm your son for warfare with Satan and his temptations is by studying God's word, the Bible, every day. Read Ephesians 6:10–17, which describes the "armor of God," with your son. Talk about each piece of weaponry and its importance in carnal warfare as well as in our spiritual battle with Satan.

Day 29: "It Is More Blessed to Give, Than to Receive"

Proverbs 28:27 (NASB): "He who gives to the poor will never want, but he who shuts his eyes will have many curses."

If you tried to count your blessings, it would take you many hours (perhaps even days) to name all the many things God has given you. If you wanted, you could start your list with the fact that God allowed you to live in the United States. Here, we live lives of luxury with all the food, clothing, housing, entertainment, and conveniences we desire. Many people in the world do not have electricity, running water, access to stores selling an abundance of food, or money to buy those products even if they were available. God has given us everything we could ever need or want, but with blessing comes responsibility. God expects us—no, commands us—to share our wealth with those who are poor.

There are many reasons to give to those in need. The first and most obvious is that it helps them. If you feed a hungry stomach, clothe a cold body, or give shelter to someone out in the elements, you fulfill his or her basic needs. But the best reason for giving to others is that it blesses you even more. Jesus says in Luke 6:38 (NLT), "If you give, you will receive. Your gift will return to you in full measure, pressed down, shaken together to make room for more, and running over. Whatever measure you use in giving—large or small—it will be used to measure what is given back to you." How wonderful! The more you bless others, the more you are blessed by God. This does not mean that you will become wealthy if you share your money with the poor but that you will receive blessings of the heart, mind, and soul.

Jesus also tells us that when we give to someone in need, even a complete stranger, it is exactly as though Jesus were here in the flesh and we were helping Him. And, conversely, when we close our eyes and ignore the poor, homeless, and sick, it is like we are turning our backs on the Lord. Jesus was compassionate, generous, and kind. He healed countless men, women, and children plagued with diseases and physical or mental disabilities. He fed thousands of hungry people who came to listen to Him preach. Jesus even raised loved ones from the dead. He performed these miracles out of love for people, to bring glory to God, and so that all men would believe that He is the Son of God and our Savior. We are to be like Jesus (compassionate, generous, and kind) today for the same reasons—to show our love for others, to bring glory to God, and to show our belief in Jesus as our Savior. When you give to or help others, they receive a blessing from you. When you help others, you receive a blessing in return. When you give, you receive. It is a *win-win* situation!

References: Acts 20:35   Luke 6:30 and 38   Matthew 25:31–46

Prayer: Dear God, giver of all blessings, thank you for lavishing me with so many material gifts here on earth. Please help me to be like Jesus—kind, loving, and compassionate. Give me a generous heart and a desire to share what I have with others. In the name of your kind, loving, and giving Son, Jesus, I pray, amen.

Parents, Talk the Talk: Read the entire passage of Matthew 25:31–46 to your son and talk to him about the importance of helping others. It is not only beneficial to us in this present life but will also be a determining factor in where we spend eternity.

Day 30: Don't Be a Spoiled Brat

Proverbs 29:15 (NASB): "The rod and reproof give wisdom, but a child who gets his own way brings shame to his mother."

Have you ever been in a store and witnessed a small child throwing a fit? Maybe he wanted a toy or a piece of candy at the checkout line and the mom said no. How awful did the screaming and crying sound to you? Can you imagine how ashamed the mother felt as he embarrassed her in front of all those people? Perhaps you even did this on occasion when you were little. But now that you are older and more mature, do you still "throw a fit" when you want something and are told no? You may not scream and cry like the toddler, but do you whine and ask repeatedly, hoping your parents will give in? If so, you have not really grown up that much. One huge indicator of how mature you are is your ability to be content with what you have. Contentment is a learned characteristic, and it means that you are happy and satisfied with your current situation. There is no question that you live a comfortable life and have everything you need. The real question is, Can you control your desires for the things you *want*, and, can you still be satisfied if you do not get them?

Before he became a Christian, the apostle Paul was probably a wealthy man. He gave up a comfortable lifestyle and material goods to serve God. He suffered many hardships, physical pain, and heartache for preaching the good news about Jesus. Yet he tells us in Philippians 4:11–13 (NASB), "... for I have learned to be content in whatever circumstances I am. I know how to get along with humble means, and I also know how to live in prosperity; in any and every circumstance I have learned the secret of being filled and going hungry, both of having abundance and suffering need. I can do all things through Christ, who strengthens me." Paul learned the secret to being content and told young Timothy, "For we have brought nothing into this world, so we cannot take anything out of it either. If we have food and covering, with these we shall be content." (I Tim. 6:7-8 NASB) He knew that God would supply all of his needs and that when He did, he should be happy and satisfied. The things we should want and strive to accumulate are riches in heaven, not more stuff here on earth.

God wants us to love Him and His Son Jesus more than money and things. We are told by the writer of Hebrews, "Stay away from the love of money; be satisfied with what you have. For God has said, 'I will never fail you. I will never forsake you.'" (Hebrews 13:5 NLT) God has given you so much. Don't be like the spoiled brat in the checkout line. Learn to be content with and thankful for what you do have, without always wanting more.

References: 1 Timothy 6:6–11   Philippians 4:11–13   Hebrews 13:5

Prayer: Almighty God, you give us everything we need, as well as most of the things we want, even though we do nothing to deserve it. We thank you for all these, but most of all we thank you for your greatest gift to all men, your Son, Jesus. Help me to seek Him and your kingdom first. Help me to love you and Jesus more than money or things. I want to learn contentment and true happiness in you. In His name, amen.

Parents, Walk the Walk: Are you content with what you have, or do you always want the most prestigious car, latest styles of clothing, biggest house, newest computer or technological gadget? Your son's level of contentment will most likely match yours. Read 2 Corinthians 11:23–28 and 12:10 with him and talk about the sparse lifestyle Paul led for the Lord. He was content in all circumstances and we should be as well.

Day 31: Anger Management

Proverbs 29:11 (NASB): "A fool always loses his temper, but a wise man holds it back."

Have you ever been so angry with someone that you said or did hurtful things that you later regretted? If so, you are not alone. Most people have done this very thing at one time or another. Since we are created in the image of God, we share the personality trait of anger with our maker. In the Old Testament, God became angry with His chosen people, the Israelites, many times when they disobeyed Him. He still becomes angry today anytime His children do not do what is right, just as your parents become angry when you disobey them.

Even Jesus, the Son of God, and God in human form, became angry on occasion. John 2:13–17, tells us about Jesus coming into Jerusalem for the Passover Feast. As He approached the temple of God, the place of worship, He saw merchants selling their wares, the money changers exchanging foreign coins, and other business being conducted. The people were not there to worship God but to buy and sell. This made Jesus very angry—so much so that He ran over and began turning their display tables upside down. He rebuked them for not showing the proper respect for the temple of God. Jesus lost His temper for a good reason. The Jews at the temple needed to be reprimanded for their dishonor of God's house of worship. Jesus did not do or say anything that was not appropriate or deserved.

It is not a sin to be angry about something if it is justified. However, if you do not control your anger but allow it to control you, then you are in jeopardy of committing sin. When you are extremely mad, do not act hastily, because you might later regret your actions. Take a "time-out" before you respond and give yourself time to think. First, make sure that your anger is deserved—should you really be angry, or did you overreact? If you are still upset, think about how you should handle the situation; seek advice from your parents or another respected adult if needed. Once you are sure of your response, then approach the offending party and try to work it out with a level head, patience, and love.

Ephesians 4:26 (NLT) says, "And don't sin by letting anger gain control over you. Don't let the sun go down while you are still angry." In other words, try to never go to bed still mad at someone; you probably will not sleep very well! If at all possible, resolve the issue quickly and make up or move on, knowing that you did your best to work it out.

As long as you live on earth, you will be faced with situations of injustice, sin, or wrongdoing by others that will infuriate you and that deserve an angry response. Anger is not sinful, but your reaction could be. When it happens, control yourself, seek advice if needed, and respond appropriately and as quickly as possible. By all means, make sure that your anger does not control your actions and lead you into sin.

References: Proverbs 16:32   John 2:13–17   Ephesians 4:26–27

Prayer: Heavenly Father, I know that I make you angry whenever I fail to follow your commands. Thank you for forgiving me when I humble myself and confess my sins. Please help me to control my anger and respond the way you would be proud of. Help me to forgive others as you forgive me. In the name of Jesus Christ, amen.

Parents, Walk the Walk: How do you handle anger? Do you fly off the handle and rant and rave, or do you keep your cool? Do you hold a grudge and give the "silent treatment" or do you forgive and forget? Your son learns anger management from you.

About the Author

I have been happily married to my husband, Jimmy, for eighteen years. I am the proud mother of two wonderful boys, ages fourteen and eleven. I have taught Bible classes for children at my home congregation, Hoover Church of Christ, for over ten years. I started writing several years ago in response to my personal Bible study. I began with a fifty-two-week devotional book for women that I shared only with my family and close friends. Soon after, I began studying the book of Proverbs. During this study, the words of wisdom spoken by Solomon to his "sons" struck my heart as they were so applicable to the lives of my own children. So I used his words as the impetus to write this thirty-one-day devotion book for boys, which has been invaluable to me as I strive to raise my sons up in the "nurture and admonition of the Lord."

I grew up in the church. My father is a minister, evangelist, and missionary. Being raised a preacher's daughter meant that I attended church services three or more times a week, as well as traveled with my dad as he preached at gospel meetings throughout the South. But it was not until I was an adult that I realized being raised in the church did not automatically make someone a Christian. Even though I was baptized at the young age of nine, I did not become committed to serving the Lord on a consistent basis until I was in my thirties. There were many times in my life that I did not live the way a Christian should. I always seemed to know a lot about the Bible because of my constant exposure to excellent sermons and teachings given by the men in my church. But it was not until I started really studying and reading my Bible every day that I realized how much closer to and reliant on God and Jesus I needed to be. When Jimmy and I were both thirty-five years old, my wonderful husband decided to become a Christian and was baptized, and I was rebaptized as an act of recommitment to the Lord. Last year, my fourteen-year–old son responded to the gospel message and was baptized into Christ as well. My heart is filled with joy knowing that I will share eternity with my family in heaven.

I am a lifelong native of Birmingham, Alabama, a true Southerner at heart. I am a homemaker and try to live my life each day putting God, Jesus, and His church first; my family second; and the world last. I enjoy any sport my boys play, Alabama football, politics, tennis, traveling, and cooking.

Bibliography

Holy Bible New American Standard Bible, Copyright (c) 1960, 1962, 1963, 1968, 1971, 1972, 1973, 1975, 1977, 1995 by The Lockman Foundation, La Habra, Calif. All rights reserved

Holy Bible New International Version Copyright © 1973, 1978, 1984 by International Bible Society® Used by permission. All rights reserved worldwide.

Holy Bible New Living Translation Used by permission of Tyndale House Publishers, Inc., Wheaton, Illinois 60189. All rights reserved. Copyright 1996.

Holy Bible King James Version

Notes

Notes

Notes

Notes

Notes

Notes

Notes

Notes

Notes

Notes

Notes

Notes

Notes

Notes

Notes

Notes

Notes

Notes

Notes

Notes

Notes

Notes

Notes

Notes

Notes

Notes

Notes

Notes

Notes

CPSIA information can be obtained
at www.ICGtesting.com
Printed in the USA
BVHW030756231120
593964BV00007B/54

9 781449 738280